Charles Borkhuis

Spontaneous Combustion

SurVision Books

First published in 2021 by
SurVision Books
Dublin, Ireland
Reggio di Calabria, Italy
www.survisionmagazine.com

Copyright © Charles Borkhuis, 2021

Design © SurVision Books, 2021

ISBN: 978-1-912963-30-0

This book is in copyright. No part of this publication may be reproduced, stored in a retrieval system, or transmitted in any form or by any means without the prior permission in writing from the publisher.

Acknowledgments

Grateful acknowledgment is made to the editors of the following, in which some of these poems, or versions of them, originally appeared:

BlazeVox Magazine: "Raising the Dead"

Brooklyn Rail: "Incognito"

Posit: "Dark Side of the Room" and "Further Instructions"

Otoliths: "Self-Reflexive Detective" and "Objects in Mirror Are Closer than They Appear"

SurVision: "Silence Is an Openness Words Can't Close"

Special thanks to: Kathleen Page and Susan Lewis.

Contents

Silence Is an Openness Words Can't Close   5
Dark Side of the Room   8
Self-Reflexive Detective   9
Incognito   19
Raising the Dead   24
Objects in Mirror Are Closer than They Appear   25
Further Instructions   39

Silence Is an Openness Words Can't Close

once put into words
something slithers away

lizard through the cracks
soon more words are needed

to fill in the crevices
where new fault lines appear

a second world climbs
upon the back of the first

forcing it forward
but once spoken things withdraw

from their names
the house boards up its doors

the period's bullet
stops the sentence in its tracks

the solution so sorely desired
now flocks around the wounded man

like birds of prey
stories from every direction

offer their succor
but as soon as they are uttered

they begin to diverge
converge and contradict

offer the dying patient hope
or dope but that is not for him

an answer now would only
shut a door on the enigma

uncertainty remains our greatest fear
while certainty makes life insufferable

one would gladly tear down the stars
like the child who perversely destroys

the castle he so carefully built
if only to stick his tongue out at it

each ending turns its back on itself
declaring *that's not what I meant*

the void sits on the end of the tongue
beseeching us to keep talking

begin again walking upon the road
to the unspeakable

mumble breath I take you for better
or worse as my own sweet vacancy

so narrow the needle
so fine the thread

silence is an openness
words can't close

Dark Side of the Room

there's another room inside this one
an anti-room with anti-matter people
sleeping or screwing on anti-matter beds

every so often someone's elbow or foot
breaks through an invisible wall
then slips back almost unnoticed

I glimpsed one of them once
staring at me bemused
like a reflection on a dark tv screen

some say the void is not empty
it's populated by virtual particles
that pop in for a quick bite and run

perhaps you're unaccustomed
to the world's indifference or phantom lovers
who annihilate each other over dinner

au contraire it gives me a certain curious comfort
to realize that I'm inhabited by beings
about whom I know virtually nothing

Self-Reflective Detective

woke up in someone else's dream
four walls white carpet and a missing roof
like the top just blown off someone's head
a giant quivering brain hovered above the fray
just to let me know it was thinking of me

it was real alright
about as real as a pair of post-surgical plastic lips
trying to steal a kiss
real as the dialogue in a trashy play
that I couldn't quite act my way out of

like every other chump on the block
I thought my thoughts were my own
but that didn't stop
someone else's words from sliding
out the side of my mouth

too much like real life to be real
never know who's doing the talking
you or some double-dealing doppelgänger
feeding you lines

everything had more holes in it
than a wiseguy's cheery alibi
tiny universes under the skin
I was riddled with them
that's how the phantoms got in

a dancing 3-legged desk here
a floating holographic ear there
I was a walking semi-permeable membrane
ghosted by a prompter in the wings

in this slice of life
the living and dead kept coming up for air
we were all amputated twitchings and stirrings
looking for a host to nibble on
while we tweeted away the midnight hour

~

someone was dreaming me
just as I was dreaming someone else
each of us was brainwashed to think
we were living out our own lives

but deep down we knew
we were all living on multiple levels at once
in some superposition until someone
observed us and we collapsed back
into a particular nobody
sipping a martini and leaning against a wall

just then I felt myself melting
through a curved bubble glass bowl
I was a rubber-lipped goldfish looking out
on a warped underwater room

I saw a hazy image of myself
like an electron reverberating
in a field of possible positions

I was standing drunk near a crazy lazy boy
waiting for someone's fat ass
to sit down and make everything right

but it wasn't right
I was aware of being awake
in a quicksand nightmare
caught in the middle of a frozen laugh
while everything and everyone
swirled around me like a bouquet of killer bees

~

dressed up as farm animals my old friends
conversed politely with grasshopper women
they all knew their lines and they knew mine
but I didn't and so was shoved ahead of myself
into a slapstick comedy of errors

my words seemed to have a life of their own
bubbling up from a multitude of voices
I looked into the mirror over a grasshopper's head
and the ghostly voices said

we're all statues around here
why don't you leave through the window
stop feeling sorry for yourself
he doesn't look like a murderer
they never do
would you recognize the dead man if you saw him again
as if I were already dead
stop reading between the lines
stop coming up roses

stop grinding your teeth
I need someone to fill in my silhouette
check please
I can't compete with busboys' toothy grins
I'm not like the others
that's what's got us worried
there's always another story inside this one
maybe but meanwhile what'll we do with the body
it'll all come out in the wash
I won't be here when you get back
you're not here now

~

I mumbled mindlessly to the grasshopper girls
as if I were talking to myself
they ate it up like popcorn at the movies
watched me making a fool of myself
playing an actor who couldn't remember his lines
a somnambulist who kept bumping
into a clutch of furniture that was trying to get familiar

I slipped into a zero-gravity lounge
and noticed it was starting to bill and coo
everything was getting a little too close
like all this was some kind of simulated sex
and of course it was

but I was looking for a little more
than the shifting veils of beauty of misdirection
reflection folded in upon reflection
I was looking for a glimmer
a clue as to what escapes the limits

what changes everything just by looking
I was waiting for a child's blindfolded kiss
I was looking for a little pin the tail on the donkey

I reached for a paperweight sun
holding down a collection of loose poems
but it burned a hole in my pocket
I was busted for trying to steal an objet d'art
they twisted my wrists into golden handcuffs

just about then mauve clouds moved in
began drizzling blood through the open roof
down the white stucco walls
where a tall iguana in a slinky red dress
handed me a transparent umbrella
her naked breasts flashed what looked like a wink
as she whipped her striped lizard tail
back and forth

you're a big talker aren't you
by the way don't bleed on the carpet
it's new

I'm not bleeding I said
the sky is falling

that's what they all say she smiled
blame it on the camel in the clouds
or a humpbacked whale scudding across the sky
won't do any good
you've got blood on your hands
you're a dead man dreaming he's still alive
it happens to us all sooner or later

that umbrella won't get you far in prison
wrong way to the sun ha ha
better get yourself a good lawyer

where are we I muttered

we're three months behind on the rent
she blew her nose in a hanky
and a fish-faced man slithered out of the shadows

you can help us he said
an index finger will be sufficient for the back rent
and perhaps a pinky for the deposit on a new roof

I struggled as iguana girl held my hand down
fish face took out a cleaver
and chopped off two of my fingers
blood spurted skyward like a screaming stallion
iguana girl stopped the bleeding
with her dirty hanky

now now said fish face *don't be greedy*
last time I counted you still had eight fingers

if I stayed there any longer
I'd be wearing stumps for hands

~

they led me to a back room with candles burning
some old guy stretched out in a granddad rocker
sipping a margarita with his shades
permanently attached to his eyeholes

look at this
a visitor awake in my dream lucid isn't it
you could be me in my mid-twenties
lost in puddle of poems I couldn't write my way out of
start with a sentence and fall on a syllable
plume to the heart just for being
it all stinks to high heaven
nowhere to go from here

I'm well versed in the drill
I see ten years written on your forehead
maybe twenty
and where do words get you in the end
I should know but I don't
not really

it's dark where you're going
maybe you'll burn all your scribblings
and quit
or not you could be me or not
depending upon
whatever

shit happens
when you're not looking
out the in-door sure
but it's not that simple
fall in with the wrong crowd
stealing from the wrong sharks
there are always consequences

the way the stray looks you in the eye
dog to dog that same

hungry growl meant to mean
pull your face out of the gutter friend

if he had a cigar he'd be your old man
another sentient being
born to feel pain or joy depending upon
what end of the night stick you're on

I stumbled into the narrow
just another self-reflexive detective
following a line of breadcrumb clues

car lights shadowed me
down a back alley wrong dream
I flashed a sunny smile
and pointed a stiff index at the hit men
for no good reason
I pulled the trigger finger
and they let me have it
punched more holes in me than a train ticket
headed to the end of the line
turned me over like a bad dream
smiling up at the abyss
I sneered it's dark in here
got a match

you want the truth
you don't have to be me
you could wake up as another someone
a poverty-stricken poet who sticks with it
to the end for no good reason
except you just might get better
or not don't laugh

that same doomed smile
on the other side of your face
is sometimes enough to keep you going

~

snuck out the front door
while the party animals were chowing down
on a delivery boy
who'd brought the wrong order

hit the street wondering
if I were still in the old boy's dream
or was this my own despoiled shore
it didn't matter anymore
the sun was pounding my temples
like a jackhammer splitting rocks
shrapnel ripped flesh off the bone
I wasn't me anymore

I never was me
but it took a bullet to tear us apart
my name peeled off my face
like a green joker's mask

I saw my doppelgänger crossing
the street without me
sound of an empty shell hitting cement

I looked into a passerby's eyes
filled with bottled-up desire
and became him or her for a few
inexplicable moments

before passing on to another
who walked away with me inside him
I was aware of being awake in their thoughts
I was the telepathic twin
of a short woman pregnant
poor and alone
should she have the child or not

sweating she turned a delirious eye
to the indifferent sun
but it came up double zeros
maybe I cried in her eyes
maybe she felt me moving inside her
maybe not

I was part of something
that was dreaming its secrets through me
joys and terrors blood sacrifices jokes
and riddles birth and death swimming
through the amniotic fluid
of a waking dream

there was no going back
I swept the sticky somnambulant letters
from my eyes the names that covered me
like afterbirth like dirt
and climbed out of the grave
one more time

Incognito

tongue-tied at the tip of a hat
the silent aperture
through which the world gets in
with its tired eyes and terrifying nostalgia
for a future that never happened

blame it on climate change
or the time it takes to become a walking cliché
I'll be the first to admit
my original is hiding out in a witness protection program
under an assumed name
in an unnamed country

perhaps you didn't notice
but I'm representing him at this very moment
same face same body parts
I'll take the double-blind pepsi challenge
anytime anywhere

finally we can say with certainty
"I am you" and who can argue
with a salient simulation that responds
to your every command
if you can't tell the difference
between your replicant's thoughts and your own
then there is no difference
be assured there are countless others
who would love to take your place

silent multiples stand in the wings
each hoping to go on
for their 15-minutes of ted-talk sincerity
finally a chance to express themselves

if only you could see the world
through my pinhole of light
everything would become clear

the problem is that there are too many stars in the sky
waving "pick me ... pick me"
too many beautiful bright-colored toys left on the beach
before the next tsunami sucks them all out to sea

the ocean eats everything in the same motion
paris floats by to take back its statue
but we all still demand more freedom
free to like free to buy free to agree
to be someone else when we leave the house

so brand me
so take my eyes with you when you go
I'm not using them

now you see me now you don't
tell it to the lost ones
squirming in the shadows under the bridge
that connects us

my tongue extended
through a slit in the curtains
to be cut loose from the next word would be enough
stop fiddling with your gadgets

when I'm talking to you
the mind is not an on-off switch

you're not really here are you
I've created you to fill a void
tonguing my ear gently a perfect hole in one
always make sure you've got enough tech up front
to avoid an accident
and subsequent scar tissue from forming

but the debt is too deep too pervasive
to clearly know what's happened
what consciousness who's lost what where
did we go I need more clarity
more time

o robot hold me close
I can almost hear what you're thinking
the future would be better without me

take my knees as collateral
I'll walk on my hands
just to keep the blood flowing

leave it to the myth-busters to twist
their facts into a more practical you
here the romantic divide
there the huff and puff of genitals
reaching for the clouds

so easily seduced by a giant ear
what you want to hear over and over
please put a stick between my teeth

and stretch me out on a board
in case I go into an operatic fit
and become a flapping fish out of water
fists in my pockets fear of drowning on air

when the curtain goes up
you must promise to play me as yourself
so as to convince the silent witnesses
the heavy breathers behind the lights
that you are me

spotlight on an adjective
nounless and flailing about on the old boards
I'll walk the plank off a drunken boat
till the ghosts come home
talk to hamlet in my dreams
miniature golf anyone

stand me up and let me think
why do golf balls look like shrunken skulls
why does the sentence flow backwards
and stop in the middle of a thought
just give me a moment to remember my lines

"alas poor yorick I knew him horatio
a fellow of infinite jest"

why follow this or that stranger on the street
or a poem through its petulant permutations
there is brain damage on the tracks

someone has fallen off the platform
someone on a train is running lines with a friend

someone has left his heart in san francisco
someone takes out her teeth and falls asleep
someone dies and is reborn as a character in a play
someone throws up in the nearest sink
someone screams a new poem from a mountain top
someone breaks for lunch
someone near tears fiddles with the buttons on her coat
someone on the street asks "got a dollar for a slice"
someone pulls a bloody someone off the tracks
someone looks into your eyes for a moment
hesitates and walks on

Raising the Dead

ropes and pulleys are working overtime
on my caged falsetto
if I were a weeper I'd weep
for all those thespians who died on stage

but I'm only a singer of songs
that's the way it is in show biz
the dancing bear and the smiling assistant
being sawed in half

then we break for lunch
soon to start all over again
putting on a face to face the public
unless you want to masquerade as yourself

a dangerous game
any way you cut it
one is always buying time
with little to show for it

the lights come up
I say my lines and die on stage
the curtain goes down
and the audience tears up

but when it comes up again the audience
doesn't want to see actors taking a bow
it wants to see its dearly departed
rising from the dead for the late show

Objects in Mirror Are Closer than They Appear

                    1

the limits talk back
like bricks in a wall like street punks
hanging out at the dead ends of sentences
like shrunken heads in birdcages
taking their revenge upon the writer
one peep at a time

everyone wants a self
they can call their own
everyone wants to unload
into a shout-box during lights out

but the writer dismisses the rabble
of inner voices as fragmented false unities
desperately grabbing for the mic
say it again

I shall not talk out in class

the sentence repeats itself
a moment before the fatal sweep
of a schoolboy's eraser
across the chalkboard

will you be my dead letter
say it again
will you shadow my pronoun
into the foaming seas

where everything starts again
as if by accident

2

o oblivion
you little talking machine
hiding under my breath

you little nothing created
for all the world to hear

the missing time of the crime
the empty space
the body left

to walk the streets unseen

when you look for me
I won't be there
when you don't look
I will
enough chitty chat
stand up and play dead

we are talking the logic
of a dream that's fled the scene

leaving a desultory detective
to decipher the trail
of crumbs
under his dining room table

3

sucking chicken bones over lunch

you think of the woman
who left you for a robot's arm

everyone's got a name
to cover for the nameless someone
that escapes them

the endless unraveling of a murder
before our eyes

I wasn't there when it happened

thinks the dead man
who ghosts the pages of a novel

the patient reader recreates
the writer's steps
slipping into another's shoes
so she may wear

the dead man's coat
his hat
while becoming a double agent

who roams the corridors of sleep
squeezing through the space
between words

4

so the world erases itself
leaving only illusions to justify
its disappearance

as if we need this second world
to claim us

I had no part in this
says the husband to his long-suffering wife

simulacra just want to have fun

it's official
the new artificial risk
promises safety within a tantalizing vision
of the animal kingdom on camera
ripping itself to pieces

playground of the near encounter
you were never really there

mother don't frighten your son

the pixelated person stands in for
a missing someone at every turn
if I have your image
do I really need you

next time I'm the murderer
following a new victim
down rainy streets

who's beginning to look
a lot like you

5

footprints in the mud
hairs in the comb

how often have I thought of myself
awake in a coma

a wife peers
into her husband's dreaming face
his muscles hanging loose
on the bone
this is the way he'll look in the coffin

let me in she whispers

but no one can enter
the dream of another

love in the background static
of the infant universe
the big bang has left us
its calling card

the dead man watches the living
from a safe distance
wondering
if they're beginning
to mean something

6

a whistle shrieks
down a lonely street

the dead man has escaped
his chalk drawing
rumors swirl
around a disappearing world

as if reality
had taken a bullet for its copy
and is now on the other side
of the mirror

your most intimate self
is a missing person

everything is safer now
that it's been screened
people too I'm so like you

now that another someone
has taken my place

but when the bandages
are unraveled
the face of the loved one
is nowhere to be found

they said it wouldn't be forever
they said his replacement
would be ready in a week

they said most people
can never tell the difference

7

everything has already happened
in an anteroom of the mind
the same characters return
in a repeating dream

the writer's wife begins to realize
she married a mannequin

the murderer has fallen in love
with his victim
who returns to the scene of the crime
to meet him for drinks

the detective sees the murderer's
face in the mirror
he shot the wrong man years ago
some fall guy took the rap

the stories keep being rewritten
the characters keep losing
their minds

whose wife left whom
who's dead and who's alive
your secret will be safe with us
it will never leave this room

but instead
melt like snow
into the carpet and chairs

8

steam rises from ancient pipes
an old guy smokes a cigar
through face towels

he's a crime writer
says everyone's secretly someone else
reader and writer husband and wife
murderer and victim
each resides under each other's skin

the person you're really talking to
left the room thirty years ago

mother don't frighten your son

we've heard it all before
the transference of a person
into a playing card

you've got the wrong man
the guilty always say that

old characters wearing new faces
the inquisition inches in
on needles and pins
the eternal return is always
just around the next corner

come closer
whose body whose smile
whose dream whose death
whose life whose gun
whose wife

9

apparently there's a black hole
in the fabric of being
a backroom where we all get to try on
various costumes and speaking parts

in this po-mo techno world
of saturation information
most everyone gets to strut their stuff
in public until they go viral
or the camera gets bored

according to the latest media reports
reality died last night
on the cutting-room floor
of a major motion picture

on another note
democracy and celebrity
walked hand-in-hand down the aisle today
they were met outside the church
by an entourage of adoring fans

perhaps it's better that way said the writer
everyone gets to play the lead in their own movie

that's easy for the writer to say
he's living off a fat advance on his next book --
objects in mirror are closer than they appear
movie offers are dangling like carrots over his head

who could want more unless
you weren't really there when all this happened

10

the detective combs the beach
searching for the missing murder weapon
listen I hear a trickle of stones
rolling past my ear
a small avalanche of words

is that you
coming back to raise the dead

the pages keep turning like endless waves
like the disappearing self or an invisible cat
that leaves its smile hanging
on the branch of a tree

one exposes the false unity of such a self
as a necessary fiction
necessary for whom
everyone who wants to remain sane

so I must take my head off
to welcome you all to the bawd and cutpurse's ball
but be warned it won't be a pretty sight

look the abandoned husband standing
on the ledge of a building has opened his arms
to the empty sky

don't jump
into more dust
the stars won't shed a tear
even if you are so elegantly dressed

look the dead man has just opened a birdcage
full of shrunken skulls
see how they fly freely over the virtual city
searching for the famous writer
asleep at his desk

11

where are we now
inside someone's book
at the outer reaches of inner space

who's speaking now
what does it matter who's speaking
the words themselves are speaking
through you through me
isn't that enough for you

but the pages are burning under our feet
put on your fire-resistant red shoes and goggles

where are we going
to the sleeping writer's house
his body is still smoking from his big ideas

the fragment will not grow past itself
it will radiate alterity from within

he made us like this
talking his criminal talk
committing his unspeakable crimes
what's left for us now

we sharpen our knives on his bones
we lick our spoons and forks over his kidneys
we eat the famous writer like a cannibal's delight

I'll start with a breast pass me a thigh
toss me a wing I only like dark meat
who's got the toes
quick before he wakes
we'll devour him without a trace

12

look how the characters keep bubbling up
to the surface as their opposites
as if no one will notice
they've turned themselves inside out

I could never do that
I could never be that person
you already are that person

look a philanderer's wife
has mistaken her husband's lies for nails
and hammered his head to the bed

look the famous writer has been driven
through an inaugural parade
wearing a crown of thorns

look the detective's body
has been dragged through the streets
by a murderous mob

look a kindly old lady has given a child
a doll's head to play with

look the murderer is having sex with his mother
correction – his stepmother
does that still count

everything counts
and everything pertains
to you

13

the detective wakes only to realize
he's been living in a recurring dream
the perfect crime that leaves no clue

but of course we know that's not true
no crime is perfect
there's always something that doesn't quite fit
like the little boy running away from home shouting

he's not my father
he's not my father

then who's that smiling man
clenching the briar between his teeth

who's that nice school teacher's wife
that replaced her husband
with a less talkative dummy who looks just like him

who's the dead man in the alley
slipping the writer a tip
about the friendly detective
who got away with murder

the unfinished novel will become famous
despite its labyrinthine loose strings
despite its characters that live inside each other
and talk incessantly about their dreams
of who they might have been
of who they might have loved
and what their lives might have meant

if only they were real
if only they were real

Further Instructions

let's say a body falls
head first into wave upon wave of roiling voices
a harsh hello here a sweet goodbye there
it all gets tangled up in the gurgle and foam
of so many swarming targets
searching for the right arrow

each to his own half-held beliefs
reincarnation placed upon a shelf
next to a can of pork and beans
a logbook of meaningful coincidences
leans against a jar of rusty keys
which door to what metaphor

no need to panic
most ideas only go so far
then someone blows a whistle
and you pick yourself up off the ground
maybe we're not made to get
to the heart of the matter
maybe nothing sticks around that long

might as well catch the next wave
of fluttering digressions or half-baked ideas
listen closely for a secret code in their banter
nudging us closer to the truth but never quite
close enough to hear matter mumbling as it turns
into light yet the transformation often occurs
while we're thinking of something else

it's no secret that words
are watching us from a distance
waiting to switch narratives or bite
maybe it's unavoidable that we are thrown
into situations that are beyond us
that we must stand for something
we don't fully understand
and act upon it with our lives

Selected Poetry Titles Published by SurVision Books

Seeds of Gravity: An Anthology of Contemporary Surrealist Poetry from Ireland
Edited by Anatoly Kudryavitsky
ISBN 978-1-912963-18-8

Noelle Kocot. *Humanity*
(New Poetics: USA)
ISBN 978-1-9995903-0-7

Ciaran O'Driscoll. *The Speaking Trees*
(New Poetics: Ireland)
ISBN 978-1-9995903-1-4

Helen Ivory. *Maps of the Abandoned City*
(New Poetics: England)
ISBN 978-1-912963-04-1

Anatoly Kudryavitsky. *Stowaway*
(New Poetics: Ireland)
ISBN 978-1-9995903-2-1

Clayre Benzadón. *Liminal Zenith*
(New Poetics: USA)
ISBN 978-1-912963-11-9

Thomas Townsley. *Tangent of Ardency*
(New Poetics: USA)
ISBN 978-1-912963-15-7

Marc Vincenz. *Einstein Fledermaus*
(New Poetics: USA)
ISBN 978-1-912963-20-1

Anton Yakovlev. *Chronos Dines Alone*
(Winner of James Tate Poetry Prize 2018)
ISBN 978-1-912963-01-0

Mikko Harvey & Jake Bauer. *Idaho Falls*
(Winner of James Tate Poetry Prize 2018)
ISBN 978-1-912963-02-7

John Bradley. *Spontaneous Mummification*
(Winner of James Tate Poetry Prize 2019)
ISBN 978-1-912963-13-3

John Thomas Allen. *Rolling in the Third Eye*
(Winner of James Tate Poetry Prize 2019)
ISBN 978-1-912963-15-7

Charles Kell. *Pierre Mask*
(Winner of James Tate Poetry Prize 2019)
ISBN 978-1-912963-19-5

Alan Elyshevitz. *Mortal Hours*
(Winner of James Tate Poetry Prize 2020)
ISBN 978-1-912963-21-8

Jon Riccio. *Eye, Romanov*
(Winner of James Tate Poetry Prize 2020)
ISBN 978-1-912963-24-9

George Kalamaras. *That Moment of Wept*
ISBN 978-1-9995903-7-6

George Kalamaras. *Through Silk-Heavy Rains*
ISBN 978-1-912963-28-7

Order our books from https://survisionmagazine.com/books.htm